AF377965

Alexander Chrzanowski

The Story of my Life and of my Fight against the Forces of Evil in the Invisible World

Éditions
Traditions & Modernité

2022

Éditions Traditions & Modernité
CP 12008
Gatineau CP de l'Hôpital, Québec
J8T 0C3
https://www.editionstm.com

The Story of my Life and of my Fight against the Forces of Evil in the Invisible World

Illustration de la couverture: iStock: « *The bright cross over clouds at sky background* ».

Titre: *The Story of my Life and of my Fight against the Forces of Evil in the Invisible World*

©Auteur : Alexandre Chrzanowski

ISBN: 978-2-925061-12-0

Dépôt légal

Bibliothèque et Archives Nationales du Québec 2022

Bibliothèque et Archives du Canada 2022

Preface

I, Alexander Chrzanowski, am writing this book so that people know everything I have done for God in the invisible reality and how I have fought evil under all its forms since the year 2002.

Since the great things I have done for God against his invisible enemies have remained secret to this day. (Almost nobody knows anything about it, since it is in the invisible reality that I have fought evil, and that almost no one can see this invisible world).

Before becoming one of the best soldiers of the Most High, I began to serve God by reading the Bible first, and to do and accomplish the good things that were written in it. I did not start differently. Those who want to become true soldiers of Christ must first study the Bible, and do what is written therein for the good.

At the beginning of my fight against the forces of evil, I was timorous and inexperienced, but the experience of 19 years of combat in the invisible reality has made me become one of the best soldiers of the Lord in the world in a fierce and merciless struggle against invisible enemies of God stronger than me.

A true Christian must consider what is invisible as

well as what is visible, because the visible universe and the invisible universe are together one and the same thing.

What exists in the visible world also exists in the invisible world. The soul of man is his invisible body. Satan and the other filthy spirits (the Devil and his angels) wander through the world in the invisible world to harm the human race and destroy souls. This is why we cannot see them: they exist in the invisible world and not in the visible one. It is because of this that many human beings do not know that they have to fight the forces of evil in the invisible world or are unaware of the very existence of demons in the invisible realm.

Sometimes demons enter into weaker people, these are the cases of possessions or infestations.

Chapter 1
The beginning

When a man's soul sleeps, he cannot see or hear the invisible world because it is asleep. But if his soul wakes up and opens its eyes, then he can see and hear what exists in the invisible reality, by the invisible senses of his soul, if his soul is still connected to his spirit.

I began to see and hear in the invisible reality thanks to spiritual mantras that I can unfortunately not reveal here, lest wicked and greedy men use them to do evil and that only makes them more powerful.

When my soul awoke, and my spiritual senses developed through these mantras, I began to understand the language of the invisible world. It was then that for the first time in my life, I saw enemies of God in the invisible world. I have seen in the invisible world a woman who had 6 humanoid bat-like demons attached to her soul by the claws of their feet; 3 on her left side, and 3 on her right side. She probably had no consciousness of that herself, like most humans who are ignorant of the existence of invisible demons, since they cannot see them. (From there might sometimes come inexplicable pain).

It was only then that I became aware of the existence of demons in the invisible world. Most of those to whom I've spoken about it didn't want to believe it, since they couldn't see these things with their own eyes, and that they have no awareness that these things really exist.

When I saw these 6 bat-like demons, it was only then that I knew for myself that these things really existed in the invisible world. Before that I had no knowledge of their existence, as it is the case for most men who inhabit this world which is nevertheless governed by the powers of evil in the invisible. (Satan and his angels.)

When I realized that the demons really existed in the invisible world, I feared in myself that they would understand that I knew they existed, and that from then on they would go after me much more than on the others who knew nothing of their existence, and that they would concentrate all their efforts against me.

This is exactly what happened: They knew that I had understood that they existed and, then they all rushed against me. From then on, I was going to have to fight them relentlessly. For the glory of God and the salvation of my soul.

At first, I was not very skilled in defeating demons. My senses in the invisible world were too little developed and my inexperience cost me enormous defeats, but God was with me, and protected me against them and lifted me up when I fell into their traps.

It was then that a Superior Spirit asked me if I swore to fight evil under all its forms, and then I answered yes without hesitation since I knew that the salvation of my soul depended on it.

I've made this promise to God dozens of times, and I've always kept my word until today. I knew that day that this would be my mission forever. Most of those who don't believe in God and who will read this book will mock me because they cannot see or hear in the invisible world and they cannot understand the existence of the invisible world, and of the things which exist there (such as the souls of men, the spirits, invisible angels, evil spirits, demons, and all variety of beings and things that exist, but which the biological eye of man cannot perceive). But I write this book anyway in the hope that the wise men who will read this book will understand and engage themselves too, as I did myself, to fight evil under all its forms.

Chapter 2
The First Battles

I was reading the Bible a lot in those days. I was no longer watching television or my music, and I no longer played my video games, because, from the beginning of my fight against the invisible demons, I was so much attacked by evil that the slightest distraction could be fatal. I could almost never sleep, and I was constantly worshiping and praising God, saying and thinking of only things that could please him, especially what was written in the Bible. I mostly read the New Testament and the Psalms of David, which I recited with all the strength of my voice to triumph over the enemies of God, for the power of God supported me against the demons and against the forces of evil. Without God, I could not have overcome evil.

My mother tolerated me saying with all the power of my voice in her house the psalms of David and other things written in the Bible because she believed in God too. I spoke to her briefly about my awareness of the existence of the forces of evil in the invisible world, and it is then that she helped me in an unexpected way: she put in my hands the marvellous red book of the Abbé Julio Houssay, Metropolitan Archbishop of France, published in 1909: the book of the Great Marvelous secrets to aid in the healing of physical and moral illnesses. I have to now clarify here that I do not claim to be a doctor, and that I do not claim in no way that I heal people, and mostly not for money. Physicians and doctors of modern medicine are useful and necessary to cure sick people, and we must not try to replace their work by prayers or interfere with the care they perform. Prayer can help, but we must let doctors and physicians do their job. The know-how of physicians and doctors is useful and necessary for the healing of the sick and the wounded: doctors and scientific doctors must be left to heal the injured and the sick themselves.

Do not take me here for a charlatan, because I do not claim to cure anyone with my prayers. I am simply trying to teach the truth of my esoteric spiritual knowledge insofar as they can be useful to those who want to fight evil in all its forms in the invisible world for the glory of God and the salvation of the world.

The book by Father Julio I spoke of has another use. He teaches that prayer can do anything, that it can obtain everything, if one asks with faith, that is to say with the certainty of having been granted, without fear, doubt, distrust or defience. Father Julio himself says in his book not to interfere with the work of doctors.

This is the power of the sons of God: What they order by word is produced and accomplished by the power of God.

As for example: If a son of God says, with power, (as in one of the psalms of David): ``Let them be ashamed and consumed altogether, those who premeditate my misfortune``, it will happen by the power of God: his enemies will be ashamed and consumed altogether. (their faces will become red of shame). Or if a son of God says: `` Arise, Lord, save me my God, you have smitten my enemies at the cheek, you have broken the teeth of the evildoers``, his enemies will have pain in their teeth and to their cheek, even if the damage is not visible to the biological eye. The sons of God are those born of Light. But be careful: you should only use this power, like the others, for good and not for evil, on pain of losing your powers. Nor should it be used to seek the glory that comes from men, or to impress the gallery, or to satisfy the curiosity of men. Jesus our Lord did not seek the glory that comes from men, but that which comes from God. This is why he commanded the demons he casted out not to make known that he was the son of God, because they knew it. This is also why often when he healed the sick, he ordered them not to tell it to anyone, because he was not looking for the glory that comes from men, but that which comes from God. If you want to know how a man can become a son of God, read the beginning of the Gospel according to Saint John, in the New Testament. Maybe you will understand.

Anyway, going back to what I was saying about the red book, I happened that I read it much, with all the power of my voice without fearing the judgment of men: It was then as if God himself put a two-edged sword (terribly sharp) on my mouth. For the word of God spoken by all the power of the voice of a man has more impact against the forces of evil, since the power of the Word thus operates with incredible power against the forces of the invisible evil. Few men will dare to speak the words of God with all the power of their voice, especially by fear of what men will think of them. I must admit that it takes a lot of courage for that, but I was one of those who dare. To sum up, the prayers and the exorcisms contained in this book had the effect of exterminating the forces of evil around me and in the surroundings, as for example, when I read the psalm of David 90, with all the power of my voice: ``You will have nothing to fear from nocturnal terrors, nor from the arrow that flies by day, nor from the enterprises of him who crawls in darkness, nor from diurnal or nocturnal demons attacks: A thousand will fall on your left, and ten thousand on your right``. So it happened. I knew and felt that thousands of the demons that were besieging me were destroyed in the invisible world round about, and they perished by the power of God, and by the Word that came out of my mouth, with all the power of my voice.

If you wonder why and how it could be possible that there were thousands of Demons who besieged me, you must know that there are billions in the world, hidden to the eyes of men in the invisible world and there are some everywhere: in the air, in the water, in the earth, in the oil, everywhere. That is one of the reasons why it is so difficult to overcome the evil forces in this world: We are from God, but the entire world lies under the grip of evil.

Sometimes they also infest men and animals; then an exorcist priest must be invited to make them come out. Real good priests can also bless all sorts of things if we ask them and make the forces of evil come out. They can also bless the fields, the animals, the clothes, the food, the oil, the drinks, the water, the earth, the houses, etc. This is why there are blessings for almost everything in the book of the Abbe Julio Houssay.

As taught in the book of Abbe Julio, the demons contaminate the air and pollute the water, in order to better carry their morbid germs; they cause injuries, they offend us, deceive our senses, mix with our blood, and are even able, within a certain limit, to introduce subtle poisons in our drinks and our food and operate all kinds of evil spells. They can even inspire bad desires and malevolent obsessions and inspire foul ideas, evil thoughts, etc. All calamities, all evil come from Satan: Satan is the enemy, there are no others. The harmful animals and insects are also forms of evil, but visible; they are the servants of the adversary.

It is also the adversary who pushes men to do wrong and who tends traps to everybody. Continuing to explain what I had to say, my prayer accomplished invisible miracles because I was engendered by God in the invisible world to fight evil and he responded powerfully to my prayers. I must say that I believed and even that I already knew that our Lord Jesus was the real son of God to an infinite degree before I had seen with my own eyes for the first time. (The other sons of God, the engendered like the real Christians, are also sons of God but to a finite degree, that means less great than Jesus himself). Among other miracles and incredible things that I saw because of my faith (Because I have seen myself many incredible things that few people have had the chance to see, and few men would believe me if I would tell them.), something incredible happened. Every time I would say some exorcisms with all the might of my voice, the tobacco toxins which were in my body would come out of my mouth under the form of a thick froth of which the odor itself reminded somehow that of the cigarette, as if all the demons were getting out of me at the microcosmic scale by the power of God. At that time I tried with all my forces to stop smoking (it was in 2002, I smoked tobacco since 1997) and I had almost succeeded but unfortunately after that I started to smoke again regularly and for that reason God punished me severely, because of all the work he had done to get out of me that abominable toxin of tobacco, that came out of my mouth through the exorcisms that I spoke of. To summarize there also happened something much more intense of which I have the honor of speaking here. I had a sublime privilege: I saw something that few men in this century have had the chance to see. I said with all my voice with a perfect faith a prayer that said: May Jesus always be in my heart and in my guts. May Jesus be all the time inside of me so that he may enliven me, that he may always be around me so that he may keep me, may he be in front of me so that he may lead me, let him be above me so that he may bless me, let him be under me so that he may strengthen me, let him be always with me so that he may deliver me from all pains and of eternal death." It is then that I saw Him! In an instant our Lord Jesus came down from above and he appeared to me. He stayed only a few seconds, but I really saw Him.

How to describe what I saw at that moment? It is as if the sun itself had entered my home, into my house. I saw the Great Light, the body of the resurrected Christ. I did not see the details of his face, neither the color of his hair, no: I saw a great magnificent and sublime light and I had never seen something so marvelous in all my life. Yes, I really saw Jesus himself. I did not have time to speak to him, neither to bow low before him, he stayed about 5 seconds only, but I will never forget it. If you ask yourself how the body of the Resurrected Jesus could have passed through the ceiling of my house to appear to me coming from above in my basement, I do not know any more than you, but what is for sure is that this Christ is living and that he radiates like the sun.

I think that the resurrected body of Christ has infinite powers, not only of healing, but also that he is almighty, like his Father, the God of the gods. For many months, I persevered in that way, trying only to please God, to do good only and to worship him continually. I slept very little and tried very hard to stop smoking tobacco…Unfortunately for me, I did with this book something I shouldn't have done. I read "The Great Ritual Catholic Exorcism of the Roman Church", the most powerful of all exorcisms of Christianity, that only the priests should use, and only for major cases…I should have been cautious of the written notice of the Abbey Julio: that only the priests shall use this exorcism and only in the most serious cases of possession, otherwise you risk to fall without defense in front of evil forces that you would have tried to fight, to overcome and to chain…Here is what happened afterwards. I read many times this powerful exorcism with great success (with all the might of my voice) and I won over against many very powerful forces of evil but after that, all the army of the Devil tried to besiege me and concentrate its efforts against me. Since those days, I have always been a case of utter fighting, that is I that I must fight more than others do in order be saved. Because even if God has edified my soul because of these grand things I did for him, evil never ceased to fight relentlessly against me, because of this "The Great Exorcist

Catholic Ritual of the Roman Church." This is why I say that if someone wants to use this book, may he use it for the good but let him not read that exorcism, neighter the heroic act prayer at the end of the book . All the other prayers in this book are not dangerous for the reader and must be used for the good only.

Because even if there has been a time when the forces of evil have left me tranquil for some years, it happened that some years later. I used again many times (with success most of the time) that exorcism, so that my name would be written in the heavens and so that God may glorify me for my victories against the demons. Besides this exorcism, I have read others, with all sorts of prayers and psalms. And I accomplished many hundreds of victorious campaigns against demons every year, while fighting evil without cease. (Fighting evil all the time in the invisible reality was my main occupation.)

 And God himself magnified me in the invisible world for each of my heroic deeds against the demons and against evil in all its forms. Strangely, many of the men who refuse to believe in God and who do not read the Bible often try to take my soul away and to grab my invisible fame from me when they see me, without fearing what God could do to them. Why don't they want to start by reading the Bible and do God's will? I did not start otherwise! What would they say if I took away what they have gained by serving money? But no, I don't want to plunder others because I like the

Good and I hate evil and I fear what the God could do to me.

After I have seen all these prodigies and that I have accomplished these great things, evil started to persecute me in all sorts of possible manners. (There is almost nothing that they did not try to make me loose my soul). The evil started to use someone who inhabited my home, but who had succumbed to the evil forces because of his weak nature, in order to harm me. That person of whom I prefer not saying the name, began stealing me regularly all my energy and my vital forces with the help of a diabolic witchcraft of which nature I do not know, and it made me fall from my innocent happiness into the misery of sin. He has stolen so many of my forces and of my life and of my youth that today, at the age of 38, I have grey hair and a white beard, and I lost my health which is ruined. Satan has immediately started to attack my spirit and to set more and more traps in front of my soul, trying to harm me by any people and all means, because he is a revengeful enemy. And though I fought evil without fearing at all his reprisals, the enemy of God did not fail to harm me in all possible ways trying, amongst others, to destroy all my projects.

I saw Jesus a second time in my life in 2003, in a place that I do not want to reveal, thanks to the same prayer as the first time. And that time, I had a little more time to contemplate him (a few more seconds).

The same magnificent and sublime Great Light . And seeing him, I felt a great happiness. An older woman was there beside me, and she saw him too. I think that she was as delighted and amazed as me, her hand on her heart.

I also, some time later, saw the Great Light which came from the heavenly Father, because of a prayer in the red book which was called "Invocations to God". That light surrounded me and rendered me delighted. I have felt a joy and an endless happiness seeing this, and I was really happy in those hours. The Light of the Father is white, and the Light of the Son is yellow and both of them are sublime. But I believe that in general the two of them together are one.

Unhappily for me, I did not find the strength in myself to renounce forever all my sins in those hours, as I should have done after seeing the Light of God and I think this disgusted him so much that because of that, that light left me and I never more had the chance to see that light again, even if during the following years there was some white light around me, because of my devotion and of the cult I rendered God. The Creator certainly expected of me, that after having contemplated his light with my eyes, I would renounce smoking tobacco for ever and also renounced to all my others little sins in order to please him, but as I couldn't, I was subjected to some sort of a condemnation. Not a condemnation to Eternal chastisement but rather the lost of the privilege of being able to see that light of God forever and it was by my own fault that it happened, because I didn't find the strength to renounce to all my sins forever.

But between 2003 and 2005, I stopped for a certain time reading the Scriptures and praying, living somehow like common and mundane men, because then I was closer to the love of the world than of the love of God. The devils and other forms of evil seemed to think I did not represent anymore a threat to them, because during that time, they stopped harassing me and they did leave me alone. I had started to smoke again regularly and to live a normal life.

Then came a day in 2005, where I paid a visit to the Priest of the Church of Sainte-Julienne at the presbytery. I spoke with him of important things, then by seeing how much he seemed happy and serene to have God with him, I decided to convert myself again and to become a prayer mill again because I wanted to be happy like him.

But the strange thing, it was a short time after my conversion that something incredible happened: it was as if all the devils had come out of hell to come and besiege me, me and only me...Why me? (I think it is then that the bad days for humanity began) Were they not in the world many other soldiers of Christ? Why did all these forces of evil came camping against me? During long months, I had to fight all an army of demons. They had assembled against me at a few kilometers at the south of the village. The priest had given me the privilege to live in the presbytery at the second floor. I had the chance to enter the church every day to worship God. So, said I, I had to fight alone against all an army of powerful and ferocious invisible devils that nobody could neighter see or hear.

This was extremely difficult for me, sometimes even beyond my strength. The least mistake was fatal. One unhappy day, I made a mistake on the battlefield and I was devoured in the invisible world by a enormous and ferocious beast...In a single instant my whole soul was devoured by that powerful demon. Instead of my soul in me, there was nothing anymore. But I did not gave up. That night, I prayed God with a perfect faith. I said to him: My God, I was devoured by your enemy. But now, can you recreate my soul so that I can fight and win over your enemies and revenge myself from them?" The Eternal greeted me. He recreated my soul exactly as it was before it was devoured by the enemy: I existed again in the invisible world, and it was exactly as it was before I was devoured.

This is one of the things I like the most with God; he is able to give back life to what is dead and even to recreate a soul who was entirely devoured. He can also do that for the physical body, it's the resurrection. God can recreate a physical body entirely even if there are only ashes left of it. It is therefore not wise to believe that we only have one life to live or to imagine that there is nothing after death because one day the dead will resurrect.

So I continued fighting evil under all its forms with ardour. With my invisible sword (because I also fought evil mostly with invisible swords), and with God's words and my prayers, and even exorcisms. During a whole night I spoke in my heart all the good words the Eternal inspired me, and till dawn, then because of a great victory against evil, a good spirit said this word that I heard: "

Death, where is your glory? Who will sing your praise?" It was precisely at the moment the sun rose. I tried to please God rather than men to the point that one day when I was at the presbytery, I was so furious to see the forces of evil winning with arrogance, and so exasperated that I dared do something that few men would do: I readed with all the might of my voice the exorcism of Leon XIII against Satan and his apostate angels, the window wide open, in order to destroy evil by the word of God. All the village of Sainte-Julienne heard the exorcism through my mouth with an incredible power.The word of God, thus used, can be felt by the forces of evil as a terrible two-edged sword very sharpened, that can separate the bones and dislocate the joints. For the forces of evil, this is an absolute terror. For approximately half an hour, I recited that exorcism with all the strength of my voice, without even fearing what men would think of me, because I was searching the glory that comes from God, and not the glory that comes from men.

But I hardly had finished reciting the exorcism that one of the sinners of the village came up to the door of my room, all scared and out of breath, while entreating me to stop. He said: "That guy, he scares people".

But it wasn't the last time that I would dare say the words of God with all my might. Before going further, I want to specify that I am not racist, neither anti-Semitic and that I recognize that Israel is the people of God. I do not hate any country, nor any government and I would never raise my hand on the inhabitants of Jerusalem because I like the Jews.

But something extraordinary happened in those days. I was inspired one day to say this word which is written in one gospel of the New Testament of Jesus, our Lord Christ. I said in his name (in french): Jerusalem, Jerusalem! thou who killest the prophets, and stonest thoses who are sent to thee! How often would I have gathered thy children together, as a hen gathers her young under her wings, but thou wouldst not! Behold, your house is left to desolate. For I say to you, you shall not see me henceforth until you shall say," Blessed is he who comes, in the name of the Lord."

And then all in a sudden, all the army of the devil who

besieged me disappeared entirely, no one was left, they were all gone! I am not too sure of well understanding what did really happened in that hour, but I am certainly not an anti-Semite and I like Israel also, but it was a great relief for me.

Another day I was passing by the small road that went from the 125 highway up to the church and as I was passing in front of the primary school Notre-Dame-de-Fatima, something impressive happened. There was an ungodly person sitting on his balcony in front of the school and I felt he was trying to take away my soul by force in the invisible world, so I dared say in a loud voice with authority this word in one of the psalms of David(in french): "May they be red with shame and let them perish all together, all those who search for my soul to take it away from me". Well, right after this man lowered his head on his breast and his face became very dark red and he moved no more. Then I continued my walk, satisfied of having been answered. It often happened that people who wanted to harm me unjustly got red with shame and also other times that people who assaulted me stepped back by the effect of the power of God who protected me.

All my efforts to stop smoking to please God were failures, even when I stopped inhaling the smoke.

Chapter 3

The ego

There also happened in those days something rather special in my life. My father brought me to a holy gnostic woman who was a teacher. (I want to clarify here that I am a Catholic Christian and that I have always been but I thought it was good in those days to enlarge my knowledge). I learned from her then her teachings about the ego (she didn't want to mean 'the thinking me' but the bad interior ego, the evil in us). She taught me we must fight the evil in ourselves. The perfect humans are those who have entirely destroyed the evil in themselves. She explained clearly that the evil in us existed under forms of heavy and dense clusters of atoms, and under the form of microscopic worms which are parasiting the body.

She showed me how the goodness in us must vanquish the evil in us. (A constant battle against the interior evil). In a certain dimension, the good in us existed under the form of a beautiful white cavalier magnificent and glaring with glory, with six arms and in his arms many weapons, including a sword, a little hatchet, a shield and an arc. And in this same dimension, evil existed in us under the form of a bad cavalier with a dark blue skin and a black beard (the evil man in us), full of shame and very ugly. He also had six arms and many weapons, of which an arc. It is what the first illustration showed. The second illustration showed how the good cavalier should defeat the evil one by tearing him to pieces with his weapons. (Unfortunatly I was never able to find those illustrations again on the internet even if I searched for them a long time but I never forgot what I had then seen). This godly and holy woman explained to me that there were 49 egos to vanquish per person, which indicates a very fierce and unequal fight. We must learn to fight evil in ourselves. She taught me also that the ego (the evil in us) existed also in a certain dimension under the form of a Medusa, a woman which hair is serpents and witch glance can change us into a stone. This is why it is so difficult to defeat our egos and many other forms of evil (it is also the reason why sometimes it is so difficult to attack an enemy of God because the gaze of evil paralyzes us and freezes us from astonishment.) When we try to destroy an evil cavalier or other forms of evil in us or outside of us, the gaze of this Medusa paralyzes us and stops us from easily getting through the other forms of evil. We therefore say that the ego paralyzes us. There are two good ways of defeating a medusa: the first is to make her to fix her own gaze with a mirror or a shield as a mirror as the hero Perseus did.(If you do not already have the necessary weapons to fight evil, ask God with faith, he will certainly give them to you because it is his desire that we fight the most of evil possible with the least help of his angels possible.) The second way of destroying a medusa, much more efficiently, is to attack it from the rear when she expects it the least and to rapidly cut its head by behind before she has the time to react. This is a technique that I perfected myself from my experience. At the beginning, it takes a lot of courage but with time, we gain assurance and we become sure of ourself. The second technique is much more efficient than the first. One day, in 2010, I accidentally harmed one of those who fought the egos (because it happens, unfortunately, that I make mistakes sometimes). And because of that later people around me seemed paralyzed. They were moving more slowly than usual, and I noticed it.

Because the gaze of the Medusa paralyzes and stun even the best warriors with stupor. The gnostic Woman also taught that the evil in us existed also under the form of a terrible hydra with seven heads that can regenerate and heal from its wounds. And when we cut one of its heads, it grows again. We therefore say here that the ego can regenerate even if it has almost entirely been destroyed; therefore it must be utterly destroyed. It is in this way that the ego in us can paralyse us and regenerate itself. She showed me an illustration in which a hero was hitting that hydra very courageously with a club. We must effectively hit that kind of monster quickly and hard, without any fear even if it a terrifying enemy. We must, like Hercules did, cut the seven heads of the hydra in a single strike so that its heads don't grow again. Understand here that these egos, that are the evil in us, are also in our daily life what pushes men to commit evil (our flaws and our bad inclinations, the iniquity and the evil in us). The bad covetousness, envy, jealousy, folly (which is always iniquity), anger, hatred, lust, laziness, greed, avarice, wickedness, cruelty, guilt, cupidity, pride, to name but a few. To work on our flaws is also a good way to win over the ego and to become humble, is another way too. For example, trying to be slow to anger, is also another way to vanquish over evil in us. Some priests of the catholic church may disagree with the gnostic teaching, but I must say here that even if I also am a catholic myself, I think it can be good to enlarge our knowledge and to assimilate the knowledge of other doctrines too, when they are useful and not to limit ourselves to study only the Bible, even if everything the Bible teaches is true and good.

If you have heard of alchemy and alchemists, you might think in yourselves that it was a vain science, as some persons say, but we must keep an open mind for the knowledge of new and ancient notions.

I personally believe that certain knowledge of Antiquity has been lost and have never been found again, especially because of the fire that destroyed Alexandria's library.

I think that the four elements of which spoke the alchemists were not effectively elements of the actual periodical table, which is scientifically exact and true. I think in fact that the four elements of which spoke the alchemists: were not elements but the four phases of matter: solid, liquid, gaseous and plasma.

Solid   =   earth

Liquid   =   water

Gaseous   =   air

Plasma   =   fire

And as for the transformation of lead into gold, I think that this means simply to transform in something good something which is bad or useless. For example to use a word or a sentence which is worthless or bad and to make something good out of it. This is also regarding the cluster of dense atoms that parasite the body which I talked about and that are also a form of ego in us.

I unfortunately cannot reveal here more about alchemy, since many things must remain concealed, and shall not be revealed, lest that evil and cupid men use it to do evil. If you find ridiculous the teachings of this book, then consider at least that nobody is forcing you to read it. I mostly care about what God thinks about me rather than what men think about me, for I search for the fame that comes from God, and not the one that comes from men. I am writing this book to be useful to the good sisters and brothers of Jesus, those who want to do good and fight against evil, and not to be admired by men. If a good and honest person wants to know the truth for the good's sake, let him pray

God to reveal it to him, and if he is a man of good will, the Lord will reveal him the way to it.

I think that this rightly resumes the teachings of the Buddha that the Asian people revere so much: The achievement of happiness and perfection, called Nirvana, is not obtained by our self-denial, but through the total destruction of the evil within us. We must completely destroy the evil within us to become perfect just as we must also destroy the evil outside of us to be saved. If a man completely destroys all his egos, then he becomes a perfect man, and he is then ready and worthy to live in Paradise, or in other worlds more evolved where evil does not exist, but it is a very difficult fight. And when Jesus says to renounce ourselves, does this not mean that we must renounce the evil in ourselves? But when someone unfortunately succumbs to evil or his egos, he falls into the power of the adversary. It is then that he becomes the slave of the evil which obliges him to do all the evil he wants. The one who has thus succumbed also begins to devour the other's souls around him in spite of himself. Evil plunges this man into degeneration, who begins to do evil deeds, often without even realizing it, as is the case of most of the ungodly men who believe there is no God.

That is why our Lord Jesus Christ said on the cross, "My Father, forgive them because they do not know what they are doing." The souls of many men and women have been devoured by the forces of evil.

The world in which we live is unfortunately governed
by Satan and his ministers, and it will be the case
until Jesus himself comes in glory with his angels, day
where the evil that is in this world will finally be
destroyed. Unfortunately, we can't destroy all our egos
in one day: It's a long and difficult fight , a fierce
struggle, especially at the beginning. Of course, it is
also necessary to combat the evil outside ourselves,
but it is also necessary to understand that it is better
to focus on defeating our own egos before applying
ourselves to fight those of others, as the parable of
Jesus our Lord, teaches: The straw and the beam:"
First remove the beam that is in your eye, then you
will see clearly to remove the straw that is in your
brother's eye. ``

It is obvious that for most men, especially for those
who work a lot, fighting their own egos and evil in all
its forms is not their main occupation. I would simply
advise them to take the time at least once a day to
fight evil, and to say one or 2 prayers and make the
sign of the cross on themselves; this helps to weaken
evil. For while it is true that unfortunately the forces
of invisible evil always come back to life after being
defeated, to fight and defeat them with a sword or
other invisible weapons weakens them considerably,
and therefore it can be said that even if demons are
still reborn after being defeated, it is still very
profitable to fight them relentlessly. The forged iron
or metal weapons can pierce and slice the demons and

also other forms of evil in the invisible. We already have the weapons we need to defeat evil, but as I have written it earlier, if you need weapons in the invisible, do not hesitate to ask for one to the God with faith, and he will grant it to you, for it is His purpose that every man fight evil. Here I want to say and repeat something very important: If you think that you lack of weapons in the invisible to overcome evil, dare to ask God with faith to give you a sword, or any other invisible weapon that you estimate useful in defeating evil, and God will certainly grant it to you, for it is God's plan that every man fight evil the most possible, for the glory of God and the salvation of the world.

When I became aware of these things (the existence of the ego which is evil in us) I understood all my faults and my flaws, and I was disgusted to see all this evil that was in me. That's when I started to apply myself to become perfect: I worked as much as possible, and I kept my home in order and in perfect cleanliness, me who previously lived in disorder and who was lazy. I applied myself to destroy and overcome my egos, and to correct all my flaws: those I was aware of.

I want to make it clear here that one must first fight and defeat the enemies of God before he can chain them. It was then that something happened that would change the course of the war I was leaning against the forces of evil. For the first time in my life, I crushed an important demon under my feet in the invisible, and I felt his warm blood under my feet. God had granted me revenge and I knew since then that every time I would defeat a demon, I would crush him under my feet and I would feel his warm blood under my feet. I must say here that this is the case every time I have triumphed over an opponent since that day. This is even the case every time I triumph over the most powerful demons. I crushed under my feet hundreds of times the dragon and the 2 beasts of which speaks the book of Revelation, and each time I overcame them, I dipped my feet in their blood after I had defeated them in the invisible. And even if the evil return to life after being defeated, they are greatly weakened by it. To dip your feet in the blood of demons after cutting them into pieces is to take advantage of a victory to the maximum. I have learned it from experience: Everyone must do their part and must overcome the as most evil and demons as possible, especially those who are more skilled than others in fighting. The experience of fighting evil is a very precious thing: In my early days, it was for me a thing incredibly difficult to overcome the demons around me. But over the years, I have acquired so much experience and skill to fight and overcome evil, that today I manage to defeat and crush the most powerful demons. I can overcome powerful demons when I do my best, because I fought them relentlessly during almost 18 years. (from2002 to 2003, and from 2005 to 2021) I myself, for the last 16 years, have crushed under my feet hundreds of times the dragon and the 2 beasts, and most of the most powerful demons in this world of evil. I crushed millions of demons under my feet in the invisible, because I have fought evil continually from morning till night all days long during the last 16 years.

I started fighting evil in 2002, but it was only in 2006 that I fought the seven-headed beast directly for the first time. On November 2, 2006, I fought in the invisible one of the most powerful men in evil in the world, but whose identity I do not want to reveal. That pleased God so much that on that day he filled me with an immense happiness. And then I felt exalted in a way that I had never been in my whole life. To such a point that I said to myself on that day: I accomplished what I had to do in this life, if I died today, I would have no regrets, because I did what I had to do. A few months later, I came to live in Joliette, in a house on Piette Street. I fought ardently throughout the days all the forces of evil that surrounded me and anything that tried to take my soul away from me. All along these days the evil one tried to grab my heart and my soul out with all his might, but I was fighting evil with an incredible skill. Sometimes evil had the upper hand on me, and the worst misfortunes happened to me in the invisible, but I did not give up even when all seemed lost, and I held on even when it was impossible, because I knew God could give me life back or recreate and re-establish my soul if I asked him in faith. And I feared nothing but the Creator and what he could do to me...

So I spent all my days fighting and defeating evil, becoming more and more skilled and experienced in the art of war against the forces of evil. Then one day did the seven-headed red dragon himself attack me directly for the first time. I was taken by surprise, because I did not expect that the most powerful of all the demons would attack me all in a sudden like an unexpected terror. It was a terrifying fight, but I fought with ardor and with all my might against this abominable dragon. (I was seeing him in the invisible, but I was mostly feeling his hatred and his anger.) I was shaking with my whole being and I was upset because of the terrors that this God's adversary poured out upon me. But I took courage, and I managed to hurt one of his 7 heads with my katana, the one that was the most to my left, because he was face to me. It was then that this terrible dragon moved away from me, a little, and it prowled to my right about 300 meters from me. Using music to inspire my courage, I came out of myself to go attack it, I crushed it and then came back into myself with caution about a good dozens of times. It was then that this dragon fled far away from me, and he never came back.

Since that day I often fought the dragon, the two beasts and many powerful demons on their own territory. Especially on days when I drank alcohol, because alcohol, if used well, can increase the strength and give courage to defeat the opponents of the Lord. But however against it is necessary to be careful not to sink into alcoholism, because it is debauchery.

Music can in some cases stimulate and give courage to overcome evil. It can push the warriors to accomplish great deeds of arms. Even when you don't understand the lyrics of a song, or even when the lyrics of a song speak of other things than fighting evil. The best example is that of some Bach chorus songs that lead me to defeat more of God's enemies than ever before, inspiring me to strike demons with my sword with strength and courage in a perfect way. But other kinds of music can also inspire to fight better: Even rap and hip-hop and other kinds of music. If you know how to use it well, you can use music to better defeat evil.

Chapter 4
The Art of Fighting Evil

We must not believe that the size of demons alone is proportional to the danger that they represent. Evil exists in a multitude of varied forms. Some demons are very cunning, and these are the ones who are the most dangerous. Even the little demons that revolve around of us alone can pose a more dangerous threat than some powerful and roaring demons.

Fighting evil is not just a matter of sword fighting: The forces of evil employ all kinds of strategies to lose us or to harm us. The most common example is temptation: Cunning demons will introduce desires and lusts in the heart of man to better harm him. They will suggest us to do evil.

For example, if someone tries to stop taking drugs, to stop drinking alcohol or even tries to quit smoking, the tempting demons will do everything they can to prevent that person from succeeding, lest that same person be released from the grip of evil on him at this level.

It is said that demons try to put souls to sleep in order that they cannot see and hear the invisible, lest that if they see the invisible, they will realize the existence of demons and then they will begin to fight the forces of evil that they see. Demons will also sometimes use other tricks, for example they will try to control the minds of men to compel them to do evil, and even mortal sins if they are able to. There are several other ways to fight evil than with the sword. For example, if a man is slow to anger, then he triumphs over evil even better than with a sword, since he who is furious commits many sins. And if a man knows how to master his mind, it's still an even a more effective thing than the sword, because he prevents the opponent from forcing him to do evil in spite of himself. But the area where the enemy is most powerful is at the level of temptation. Demons arouse lusts that feed the rot of this world. They will inspire bad desires that will push man to seek more and more money to satisfy his desires, going so far as to push them, in some cases, to commit crimes. For example, a man who has an addiction to strong drugs, goes sometimes so far as to steal, and even kill to get his dose, and some women will go to the point of prostituting themselves to get what they desire or want. We still have to be careful not to despise others too much by judging them harshly. We can also be tempted ourselves, and even if we do not have one defect, we still have others. There is no one utterly just in the world, and there is no one who does never sin. One may be tempted to despise someone because he has a flaw that he does not have himself, but will he not be less contemptuous of someone who does the same thing as him? For example, a non-smoker may easily despise someone who smokes tobacco, while one smoker is not going to despise another smoker because he smokes too. But doesn't this same non-smoker also have some flaws in himself? One of the most difficult ways to overcome evil is to resist temptation: it is to fight the enemy on its own ground. You also have to be very careful even after defeating evil, or even after a great victory against the opponent. We must be very careful. Evil is also, as I said earlier, like a hydra whose severed heads can grow back, and the ego itself can regenerate, even after being almost completely destroyed. Defeated demons can come back to attack us even if they have been weakened by the fight against them. For example, if someone says the Lord's Prayer, he says at the end of his prayer: "Do not let us succumb to temptation, but deliver us from evil", he does well to believe that it has been answered. But if immediately after he imagines that evil will leave him alone, that there is no longer any danger and that he lowers his guard imagining that no more evil will attack him, and that nothing can happen to him anymore, he commits a very serious imprudence, and he will eventually be affected by it anyway. Yes, the Father can deliver him from evil, but the person must still continue to fight evil even if it seems to him that it is no longer necessary. For example, if a reckless man imagines that he no longer needs to fight evil just because the Son of God Jesus came to earth to erase sin and to destroy Satan's work and that he imagines that the fight against evil is over, he then ignores a real danger. By ceasing to fight evil, he not only opens the door to all that is against God, but in addition he exposes himself to leaving the enemy a hold on him. And the enemy will not fail if he is able to, to seize the opportunity to try to force him to commit a mortal sin if possible to drag him into eternal death. We really have to consider the danger as being real. Ignoring the existence of the forces of evil is very dangerous and perilous.

I was saying that it is at the level of temptation that the forces of evil are the most powerful but we must have a good will. You really have to be very resilient, but with time you end up used to pain and misfortunes. For example, someone who begins to fight evil will be less efficient at first because of the misfortunes that the war against evil will attract on him, while at the end, he will be able to endure everything; but he must persevere and hold on anyway until the end AND NEVER GIVE UP. It can often happen that the opponent, being powerful in this world, inflicts calamities on us and attracts great misfortunes to us, and even sometimes it seems to have even made us lose our soul, but we must never give up, and always do our best to be saved despite all the abominable misfortunes that can bring us down. You have to hold on until the end to be saved. You must never get discouraged either because it would be as if you surrendered your weapons to the enemy. You must always be on your guard not to let any access to the forces of evil of whom the principal aim is to drag the most possible souls in eternal death. You must hope even when all seems lost, saying:

NO, NEVER WILL WE ABANDON THAT FOR

WHICH WE HAVE FOUGHT AND SUFFERED, NEVER!

But if we have the good will, which the demons cannot overcome, we must also know how to NOT FEAR CORPORAL DEATH, in the sense that no one should not fear what evil could do to us. We must fear only God alone because it is he who decides who will live and who will die eternally. I was talking earlier about the fact that the size of demons is not always directly proportional to the danger they represent, but it is also because evil exists in a multitude of forms, and not only in the invisible. Criminal gangs of evildoers are a visible form of evil, and the good police officers are tasked with protecting us against them. Evil sects and cults are also one of visible forms of evil. Harmful insects and harmful animals and even some harmful viruses and bacteria are also forms of evil in the visible. We can fight them in many ways in the visible too, but we must not violate the law of men.

Chapter 5
The Visible and Invisible Reality

Many human beings seem to imagine that they only have one life to live, and they don't think at what will happen to them after death. This is serious foolishness. Life in this world is a very short experience but of paramount importance for the eternal fate of man: Those who have done good will go to eternal life, and those who have done evil will go to eternal punishment. Many people think that hell does not exist, that God does not exist, and do not know that they must fight evil. But God is intelligent: If prisons exist, well hell does exist too! Some men also have a misconception about paradise and hell. Some people seem to think that hell is a big party where we have fun, and that paradise is a boring place on the clouds, where there's nothing else to do but play harp!!! What foolishness!!!

Hell is a horrible and terrible place where those who have been evildoers are consumed eternally, a place where the fire never extinguishes, and where gnawing worms never die, and everything must be done to avoid ending up in it! It is God Himself who judges and decides who goes to heaven and who goes to hell, and it is the angels of God themselves who carry to paradise the pious souls of the saints, and who throw into the fiery furnace the wicked and the evildoers. And the Adversary himself will eventually burn there eternally, he and his evil angels who are against God! Some think that there are several kinds of paradise and several kinds of hell and purgatory, and I believe it too. I believe that not all purgatories are the same. I think that some souls are sent to purgatory for a certain time only, and then after being restored after having expiated their sins.

The best of paradise is probably reserved for the most righteous, and the worst punishment is surely reserved for the worst criminals. I think paradise is definitely worth suffering and fighting for God. Personally, I obey to God above all by fear of his punishment, but with the hope of living in paradise forever.

But if some evil men deceive themselves and imagine that there is nothing after death, it might also be because they know that they will have no hope left when the thread of their corporal life will be cut off, for they will then descend to hell, and will not have a share in the resurrection with the righteous men. It is also necessary to understand one thing: On the day of Judgment, after the end of the world, men will be resurrected and be held accountable for their actions. Those who will have done good will go to eternal life, and those who have done evil will go to eternal punishment.

To be saved the most important thing is to be careful not to sin against the Holy Spirit, for it is a mortal sin that God will never forgive. You also have to be careful not to worship another God than the Creator, because God destroys idolaters. Then finally, you also have to do everything to save your soul and spirit, while avoiding to commit serious misconduct. As Jesus says in the Bible: "The wicked will be thrown into the fiery furnace, then the righteous men will shine like the sun. ``

As far as I am concerned, I chose to fight against evil until my death and to do everything I can to gain eternal life. I have a lot of experience fighting evil, but sometimes it's still very difficult to overcome the demons. It is a difficult war without mercy that must be waged against the enemies of the Lord until the evil be completely destroyed forever. Yes, it can be good to live your life to the fullest, and even if it can be good to enjoy it a little, we must never forget what is most important: To do good, to fight evil and to do everything we can to be saved and to gain eternal life, and to avoid eternal punishment.

We must beware of the ungodly men of this century: They will plunder you in the invisible, they will tend traps to your soul, by greed, without even fearing God's judgment. They even will try to destroy your faith to make you more vulnerable targets.

As David's 1st Psalm says: "Happy the man who follows not the counsel of the wicked. Nor walks in the way of sinners, nor sits in the company of the insolent. But who delights in the law of the Lord and meditates on his law day and night."

For those who will start fighting evil, it will be very

difficult, especially at first, but they will have to persevere, and over time they will get used to suffering, and in the end, they will be able to endure almost anything. You have to be resilient. Sometimes it is necessary to attack and strike hard evil without fear of reprisals, but at the same time, we must be extremely careful to prevent evil from reaching us, and this requires extreme vigilance.

Beware of yourself when evil attacks you, to prevent it from dragging you into eternal death or from making you lose your soul. The forces of evil will do all that they can to prevent you from saving your souls, they will try by any possible means to lose you, such as, for example, they will try to force you to commit mortal sins or forcing you to worship infamous idols.

This war against evil began when Lucifer (Lucifer means bearer of light), the most powerful angel in the universe, and God's favorite angel, desired to become God Himself. He became the prince of pride and the prince of darkness, saying, "Who is like me? ``He wanted to take the Throne of God and reign in his place. It is then that by his fault that the third of all the angels of the universe (one-third of the stars and of everything in the universe) were seduced by him, and joined him in a rebellion against God. It is since that time that we have to fight the principalities and powers of evil, the evil masters of this world of darkness, and evil spirits spread in the heavenly places. Then the archangel Michael, the protector of the Living God, said: Micheas, Micheas (which means who is like God!) to bring as many angels as possible back to obedience to God. And the other two-thirds of the universe remained faithful to the Creator. Many of the angels Satan dragged into his fall were of a nature superior to that of man. (In power and intelligence, among others.) That's why the angels of the Devil are so cunning, and sometimes so difficult to overcome. Thus began the Great War between Good and Evil, between God and Satan. It is said of the Adversary that he is an ancient enemy because this war began a very long time ago. But the world in which we live is unfortunately currently ruled by Satan, until Our Lord Jesus comes in glory with his angels, to purify the world by fire, as God did by water in Noah's time. In case you wonder why this war against evil is not already over, since two two-thirds the universe have remained faithful to the Creator, let it be known that it is because the two-thirds of the universe that have remained faithful to the creator are not entirely composed of angels who are charged with fighting evil. There is in the kingdom of God a hierarchy of angels and higher spirits, and they are not all put in charge of fighting evil. It's the archangel Michael himself who is charged with commanding the Lord's heavenly militias, and it is also he who is responsible for protecting God against Satan. And I try to help the archangel Michael against the forces of evil that still dominate the world. This is a very merciless and intense war, and it has been raging since immemorial times.

That's why we fight.

Astral travelling, as it is called, is common for those who are experienced in fighting evil. For me to get out of my body to face and crush demons outside of me is a common thing, which I do several hundred times a day, especially to face evil on its own territory or around me.

Getting out of your body and exploring the universe can certainly be a fascinating thing, but you have to be careful: when man's soul comes out of his own body, it becomes more vulnerable to the attacks of evil, because the body protects the soul that is in it. And you must not forget to come back in yourself after!

Those who hear voices are not all schizophrenics. Some people are simply hearing spirits or souls talking in the invisible world because their sense of hearing is awakened in the invisible.

Those who evoke the dead or who play ouijah commit a serious imprudence. God does not want us to talk to the dead, because they have the right to rest in peace. And those who play ouijha attract almost all the time on themselves evil spirits, bad ghosts or even larvae, which feed on their vital forces: It is very dangerous to play ouijha and thus allow evil spirits to enter us.

Fighting Death is something very difficult. To overcome death, when confronted, you must, above all, have no fear of dying, because it is by this fear that death has control over us. The best way to defeat death is to hit it on the neck. From left to right. The best way to beat a seven-headed enemy is to hit his heads from left to right, but one can take initiatives sometimes, and experienced warriors develop their own methods. Some huge demons are easier to defeat if you hit one of its front legs. The blood of death is black. The blood of numerous demons is black but many have dark red blood.

I was talking to someone who was with God, but whose identity I don't want to reveal. I was telling him that I was very saddened to see that a multitude of the inhabitants of the world were doing wrong and committing mischiefs without fearing God at all, and I told him that I feared for their salvation. So, he said, "Oh, you know, they are going into hell through full doors." I think he was unfortunately right, but that was in 2005. When evil (god's enemies) will have disappeared from the world, there will be no more suffering, no more famines, murders, wars, neither theft nor crimes, as in some worlds more evolved in the heavens, where evil no longer exists. Personally, I don't believe there are too many humans beings who live in the world, but rather that there are too many human beings doing evil in the world. I believe that the three greatest religions have the same God, who is the Creator of the universe. Indeed, the Christians, the Jews and Muslims all agree that the Creator is the God of all things and that there is no other than him. But I personally believe that the best religion is esoteric Christianity.

I have never given up the fight against evil since 2005 until today. (2021). For those considered as warriors of the Lord, during a fight, the defeat of the forces of evil can become the only goal. Remove all pity or compassion for opponents of God. Kill all the invisible enemies of God who stand against you, even if it were the Dragon or the Beast itself. The truth lies at the heart of the art of fighting against the forces of evil. In 2007, while I was living in Joliette, the enemy entered me to try to possess me. I had to use more than 30 exorcisms to get it out of myself. But I know that there is nothing unclean in me. I found in 2005 an invisible katana in a blacksmith shop who was very skilled at making samurai swords, but I am a rather a warrior of the ronin type.

One day I risked my life for The Lord, and then I actually heard His voice tell me with a solemn tone: "Do not seek me among the dead, but among those living." This is the only time in all my life I had the chance to hear his voice. In 2008 I fought the beast hand-to-hand throughout the days with my sharp scythian and my very large sword, two weapons that I had asked for and obtained from the Lord, because these weapons were more effective than my katana to inflict deep wounds on larger demons. And God in those times filled me with glory and goodness to reward me for my great deeds of arms. I also led several successful campaigns against all kinds of forms of evil.

I saw the moon red as blood and huge in the sky on May 18, 2008. I believed then that the end of the world had come, but it was only a sign from heaven and not the last day as I thought. There was also a huge fire lit far away, but I didn't know what it was.

From 2008 to 2012 I lived in St-Charles-Borromée, then in Saint-Thomas-de-Joliette from 2012 to 2021, where I didn't have access to the internet, but during all those years, I fought evil without cease from morning to evening throughout the days.

There are no victories without fighting. The Lord Jesus said, "It is difficult, certainly, but if it was easy, what glory would there be in doing it?" Especially read Isaiah chapter 8, verse 19, so that you never suffer from anxiety attacks again. I became aware of this in 2007, and since that time I have almost never had an anxiety attack. That is the most useful thing in the entire Old Testament, in my opinion.

And if, when you fight evil, you get discouraged because no one sees what you do, or because the bad guys seem to triumph with impunity in secret and succeed in their enterprises, know that there is nothing secret that will not be known, and nothing hidden that will not be revealed on the last day.

Here are some proverbs that come from me: Even if we cannot predict the future, we see, in the way things happen, that an Incredible unprecedented disaster is about to happen and surprise humanity.

The man's state of mind can alter reality.

A man cannot lift the sea, nor know all that it contains by probing it.

When a man wonders why he is on earth, he forgets that it is to fight evil; it is then that evil comes and pierces his heart and that this man becomes depressed.

Soon it will be frowned upon to pollute, as a shameful vice.

Things in the world will get worse and worse until disaster.

Money alone does not bring happiness. Don't live your life by relying only on material wealth. Search for happiness in God.

An invader's purpose is revealed by his actions on the battlefield.

Sometimes the happiness of some can also make the happiness of others.

The more evil is destroyed, the better the world will

be.

The more wise persons there are, the least hard life will be.

End

Chapter 6
Guidelines and tips
for
spiritual fight

Here are some guidelines and tips that can help you fight better and make yourselves better Christians and warriors:

X: Tips for being just:

It's just me against evil

Let the God be, let the good be

Love what Christ loves

Hate what Christ hates

Protect what Christ loves

Attack what Christ hates

Love what the creator loves

Like he loves it himself

Hate what God hates as He hates it

Fight Satan as God wants you to fight Satan

Fight evil as God wants you to fight evil

Do the good as God wants you to do the good

Do what God wants you to do

Love God as he wants to be loved

Love the Father as Jesus loves the Father

Love light as God loves light

Do good to the sheep

Love the others as God loves them

Respect life

Protect the kingdom of heaven from those who tear it up and assail it with violence

Break the fingers that take things in your heart

Protect the Lord's sheep

Attack the evil wolves

Attack the wolves that are disguised as sheep

Do not give what is sacred to dogs

Do not throw pearls to the pigs

Attack the demons

Dare to defy the evil and you will be glorious

My son, listen to my advice

Loving God and your neighbors is the whole law

I don't love God if I don't love my brother

There is no other heaven but to love

Collect a treasure in heaven

Near God, where thieves do not steal

And not on earth

For where your treasure is

There too will be your heart

Fearing the Lord is the main point of science and the beginning of wisdom

And the first degree of humility

Don't read the Bible too much

Love the light

To love means to have happiness

And to fear god is to hate evil

Sacrificing your corporal life for those you love

This is the noblest sacrifice

Be pious and honest

Do not covet the property of others

Don't go to your neighbor's wife

Beware of flattering words

Don't drink too much beer or wine

Love good, hate evil

Read Solomon's proverbs

Go into the light

Ask the angels for protection

Ask them to take you into the light

And to take you to paradise

Keep your heart more than anything else you keep

Direct your heart, master your mind

And invoke God in distress; be like the knight who
challenges the dragon in his lair

Pay God the tithe and the first fruits of your income

And you will be prosperous, and your cellars will be
full of pouts

And your granaries full of wheat

Study the Catholic religion

And the other spiritual sciences

Especially esoteric Christianity

With the fear of God, who is holy and who always
subsists

Welcome the light and word of God

With a loyal and good heart and do your best to understand its meaning

And you will be able to bear fruits of all kinds

Abide in Jesus, the vine of which we are the branches

And it will prune you and you will bear good fruit

Amen, Hallelujah!

Invoke the Holy Spirit

And ask him

To enlighten you in your reading of the scriptures

And even in the midst of the worst dangers

Be like the dove with silver wings,

with a back shining like gold.

You must enter the white lodges,

and commit to fighting the black lodges

You must commit to fighting evil in all its forms.

If men do evil in spite of themselves because they have succumbed

Fight then the evil that forces them to sin.

II: How to fight

I attack the evil that surrounds us!

I attack the evil that try to fool us

Me what I have I hold it firm

Arm yourself against evil

Take on the weapons of justice

Eye scornfully those who spy on you

Kill your enemies

Attack the evil underworlds

Go up in the heavens

Attack your egos

Fight especially also the evil in you

The good man in you must kill the evil man in you

The good cavalier in you must kill the evil cavalier in you

Evil in you exists in three forms

The evil knight (who has 6 arms and several weapons including a bow)

The medusa whose gaze paralyses

And the seven-headed hydra that regenerates.

Attack hydras with a club

Or slice his seven heads in one blow

Strike it fast and hard

Be merciless against evil

No, it's not over

Remember that you must fight evil

In all its forms

There are 49 egos per person

But the valor is superior to number

However, victory is assured

You can't defeat them all in one day

Seek the glory that comes from God

Not the one that comes from men

However, good reputation is better than gold and silver

Our works will be praised one day

The good cavaliers (us) who fight the ego have 6 arms and several weapons

Including an arc

They are bursting with glory and ride a white destrier

Protect them against evil

They will win this war

Egos are clusters of very dense atoms that parasitize the body. They exist in a certain dimension in the form of evil cavaliers (the bad man in us) they have dark blue skin, and are dressed in black, they have a black beard, and they are covered with shame and are very ugly.

They have 6 arms and several weapons including a bow

The good cavalier must cut the evil cavalier into pieces

Egos paralyze us

If they paralyze you, cut off the head of the medusa from behind, without ever staring at her glance because it would paralyze you or use the mirror shield like Perseus and make the medusa look at her own gaze in the mirror of your shield. (When evil looks at himself in a mirror, his glance itself stuns him).

Do not hesitate to strike evil hard

You might manage to fight only one enemy at a time

But sometimes you can throw yourself on a whole bunch of enemies

And overcome them

Be always on the good side

And fight evil in all its forms

Hate iniquity when it comes to you

You have to fight evil to go to heaven

You have to overcome evil to be good and happy

The purpose of this book is to teach you

To fight evil in all its forms

You have to train first

You can become a warrior of God

But you have to work hard and persevere

And, to the extent that it is humanly possible for you, to definitively renounce evil.

(Read Jesus' teaching to fight evil.)

Put God's words in your heart, so that you do not sin against Him

We fight not against men, but in general against the principalities and powers of evil and darkness, against the evil masters of this world of darkness.

And against the spirits of malice in the air and other forms of evil; they are everywhere Including the ego (the evil in us) that paralyzes us.

Pray to God that he provides you with the necessary weapons for combat

The less you fear corporal death, the more effective you will be in facing the horror of evil.

However, be careful at war

I made of fighting evil a priority

On all sides, evil rises against us to lose us

Because Satan and the other filthy spirits wander throughout the world to harm mankind and lose souls.

Constantly standing on guard

Even when sleeping we must fight evil

Crushing all of Satan's power under our feet (after defeating them)

Crushing all traitors of misfortune

And all the demons, the bad snakes, the scorpions the wolves etc.

Attack all forms of evil

Go out, attack your besiegers

Protect the good against evil

The katana was the weapon of the samurai

Ask God for one

There are always demons around us to fight

It's up to you to find them and defeat them

Wheel with all blows evil and the enemies of God.

Stay firm with the assistance of the Most High

He will instruct his angels to Keep you in all your ways

They will carry you in their hands

Lest you hit your feet against the stone

You will walk on the viper and the scorpion

And from the heel you will hit the lion and the dragon

He will shelter your head on the day of the battle

Fighting evil in all its forms is our duty, it is my job.

The kingdom of God is assailed by the powerful and the violent of this world

We are attacked by evil and by vice

Always be on your guard

Don't be troubled

Fear no evil

And watch behind your back

Because some enemies strike from behind

It is the violent and powerful of this world who are tearing the kingdom from heaven.

Fight those who with violence are grabbing away the kingdom of God.

Do not hesitate to hit evil hard

Be merciless against evil

Don't forget; God will always be with you

For the Lord keeps you

WORK HARD TO FIGHT SATAN AND HIS ANGELS AND EVILDOERS

Keep peace in your heart, avoid evil, do good

Seek peace, pursue it.

To have peace, one must first defeat evil and the adversary.

For before putting peace in a place,

God makes war against evil there.

The one who seeks peace

Must prepare for war (because of the enemy)

Even if you think it's over, keep fighting evil and being on your guard

Let God guide your hand and act in you

We are of God

But the whole world lies in the grip of the evil's power

You are conquerors of evil and the truth is within you

Walk in the light, stay in the light to be sons of the light

Fight the battles God wants you to fight

Do all the good God wants you to do

Earn your living honestly

Remember, it is also God in you who fights evil;

Fight using his energies if he wants to

Let us glorify God, it is just.

When you will be able to, protect God against evil

So that evil disappears entirely from the earth.

If you can say Jesus Christ is the Lord, it means that the Holy Spirit is in you.

Never let your soul sleep, tell it to watch over you while you sleep.

The slightest distraction can be fatal.

Avoid throwing pearls at the pigs

Sing praises to God

And the psalms of David by fulfilling them for the good

Read and practice Jesus' teaching

And those of its laws that concern you

Catholic doctrine is certain and truthful

For those considered as warriors of the Most High

During a fight

Defeating the forces of evil can become the only goal.

Remove all mercy or compassion for God's enemies

Kill all the invisible adversaries of the God who stand against you,

even if it were the Dragon or the beast itself.

Truth lies at the heart of the art of fighting against the forces of evil.

Keep your heart more than anything you keep

Hold your mind

Keep yourself from the bad

With God's Help

Possess your soul through your patience

Direct your heart to fight evil

Possess the peace and glory that comes from Jesus (the one he gives you.)

The heart of the warrior of light must fear only God alone

because the punishment is in his indignation and life is in his good will.

Brother or sister, I urge you to read the Scriptures and put them into practice

Remove all compassion for demons, find them, defeat them and crush them

Protect your head, your neck and your heart

Evil exists in many forms

You have to count them, isolate them, delete them, and crush them to the last one.

Don't let any of them escape.

Only the elite warriors knows how to fight

Evil in all its forms without making mistakes

To learn you must first train

Start by fighting the demons closest to you.

Open your mind and pray to the Lord

Meditate on his law day and night

Then the Creator will show you the way to heaven

But first you have to attack the inferno and the Hades

(Ask God for help from His angels when evil seems to be stronger than you)

And defeat evil

Invoking God

God spoke to me only once, and I really heard His voice tell me

DO NOT SEEK ME AMONG THE DEADS, BUT AMONG THOSE LIVING

And I testify for having seen a great light

In which is the perfect true happiness

HE IS THE GOD OF THE LIVING

Detach yourself from your bodily life and from the matter

Don't get bogged down in the matter

You will often be crucified and persecuted in the invisible

True happiness passes through the cross

The crux of light and love

Follow Jesus to be worthy of Him

Invoke him by saying

May Jesus always be in my heart and in my guts

May he always be inside me so that he may vivify me, may he be around me so that he may keep me, may he be in front of me so that he may lead me, behind me so that he may guard me, may he be with me that he may govern me, that he may be above me that he may bless me; may he always be with me so that he may deliver me from all sorrows and eternal death. Amen

NEVER GIVE UP EVERYTHING YOU FOUGHT FOR, NEVER!

Never get bogged down in matter

Communion gives great strength

Drinking gives courage and calms pain

But don't drink too much

The temptator tries to get our mind bogged down in matter

Courage can be learned

Detach yourself of your corporal life when you fight

But be prudent at war

Don't be afraid of injuries

Watch your back often

Protect God's armies

Against the forces of darkness, if you can

Also, invoke angels when in distress

: Michael, Gabriel, Raphael and Uriel

Or other angels if at least you know their names

Be like a knight; always be kind, good and lovable

Do not take revenge on men except when they are
against God

Love the good and hate evil

Attack the entire army of the devil

The Holy Spirit exorcises the ego

Cast out the demons and diseases by The Lord

With faith and prayer

In the morning, visualize the pyramids of Kheops

Don't listen to the voices of magicians and enchanters

Spit flames on those who harm you in the invisible

 if you know how to

Do good, avoid evil

Beware of what is immoral

Attack the evil powers of the earth...and of hell

Attack the evil ones who control this world in the invisible; attack the enemies of Jesus

But do not violate the law of men

Respect the right authorities

Because Jesus helps them to maintain order

The fate of Satan and his evil angels

And the ungodly evil men is an inextinguishable fire with worms that never die (manage yourself not to end up in there)

Like an eternal death into which Satan wants to drag us

Satan has claimed you to sift through you like one sifts wheat

Stand on your guard, resist him, watch out not to let him overcome you!

He wanders like a lion looking for who to devour

Resist him and he will flee away from you

Satan is the enemy, there are no others

I have already done a big cleaning with other angels

But there are still many demons left to fight

Do what is good; it will keep them away

Fight Satan on the grounds where you can defeat him.

But sometimes it will be necessary to hold difficult positions:

A brave man may fall, but he cannot yield

Protect the good ones against the evil ones

And protect those who are for Jesus

Against those who are against Jesus (in the invisible reality)

Attack the evil idols

But don't plunder their temples

Don't let the darkness invade you

Don't let the evil win

Attack demons and all other forms of evil

Get prayers and exorcisms to fight them like for example Abbe Julio

Beware of the carnal men and of the evil looters

We must fight evil so as not to be devoured

You have to fight evil all day long

We must fight evil with the Lord at our side

Fight evil with the help of your allies

Fight evil with the help of God's forces and let him guide your hand

Because fighting by your own strength means exhausting yourself

Be on your guard all day long

Invocate the God of peace, his angels and the living saints for their assistance on

the battlefield

Take initiatives sometimes

Of strength and courage, you must arm yourself

Against the principalities and powers

Against the evil masters of this world of darkness

And against the spirits of malice spread in the air

They hide everywhere: in salt, in water, in the earth, in oil, in air etc....

Their throne is in Pergamon,...

Do not fear for your life, protect your neck, do not fear to suffer for the good.

Acquire resistance to pain

Each of your hairs is counted

Fear not ... God will protect you.

Fight the demons to the last

To defeat them, you do not need to be a veteran

You just have to train to fight and to have courage

The story of a young warrior

Since 2002

He fights evil

Detaching himself from his life

To fight evil

Willing to sacrifice

To obtain victory

By any good means

Ready to suffer everything

Without ever giving up

It's the story of a young warrior

Named Alexander

Who fights for God

Ready to expose himself to all dangers to help

humanity in peril

He was not afraid to defy evil

Following the Way of the Cross

For often they persecuted him in the invisible

But still he stands firm

With decisive blows of his scythe and his katana

He beheaded the heads of the beast and those of a
bunch of hideous seven-headed

monsters and of many powerful demons.

Liberating humanity in this way

And thus saving many souls

He doesn't want to stop fighting

As long as the war against evil will last

No mercy for the evil

Detach yourself of your corporal life

Fighting Satan and his angels

Destroy the angels of evil to the last

Until total peace returns

But victory loves prudence

Destroying demons

Make heaps of them

Don't let any of them escape

Exterminate evil and vermin

Fight the bad dragons, bad snakes

And the evil principalities and the evil powers of this world of darkness

With your heart pray

Give yourself good orders in your heart

Talk to yourself in your heart

Meditate on God's law day and night

All the good that God wants you to do, do it

Fight the battles God wants you to fight

Strike of all possible blows on all the demons

Fight evil without fear of its reprisals

Know that if demons kill

Or devour your soul, God will recreate you

Or resurrect you, if you ask him it with faith

And God always restores those who love Him

Weigh the good words and keep them in your heart

III Good advice:

Hit the demons, hit the evil ghosts

Power to the good ones

Death to the devils

Protect those who protect God

And your protectors against God's enemies

Protect good servants

Feed those who are hungry

Weigh your words

You will see that good words are precious things

That you must understand and keep a loyal and good heart,

and that you must put in your heart so as not to sin against the Lord,

and in order to bear good fruit

Take the lead in killing the sellers of death

Blow the devils with the burst, inside and outside

Learn how to use all kinds of weapons to defeat invisible demons.

Win this war for God

Conquer this world for Jesus

Until when will you sleep, lazy man?

Fight the bad guys in the invisible

Hunt down demons

Hit evil hard

Do not hesitate to face and attack the enemy

Go to the Living God

Look into the living god (into the light of God)

Never look into death

You would be plunged into darkness

Read mostly Isaiah chapter 8, verse 19, that says:

And when they shall say to you: Seek pythons and diviners, who mutter in their enchantments. answer:

Will not the people rather look into its God? What? To go the dead for the livings!

Look into the living God

It's your destiny to be saved

Don't go to the dead, never

Stay in the light

The Warrior Code

Read the Bible and do God's will

Read David's psalms to fight evil

Seek peace, pursue it

Look at the honest man

See the righteous men on earth

There is a posterity for the peaceful man

But the bad guys end up being entrenched.

Never worship gods other than the Creator alone

For he is a jealous god and he destroys idolaters

Never accept the vile mark of the beast on you, and never worship the beast and its image

And keep yourself from idols

DON'T OUTRAGE YOUR NEIGHBOR

DON'T HURT OTHERS

TRUE HAPPINESS PASSES THROUGH THE CROSS

THE CROSS OF LIGHT AND LOVE, IF YOU

SUCCUMB, ASK FOR REPENTANCE

AND FIGHT THE FORCES OF DARKNESS

AQUIRE RESISTANCE TO PAIN and make it operate

Fight the bad warriors of the shadows.

Protect wisdom and intelligence

Acquire from God wisdom and intelligence, which are the two most sublime things in the

universe.

The war:

I check my weapons

I gird my swords at the side

And I attack Babylon

I got my katana

From one of the best blacksmiths in Japan

I learned martial arts like a ronin

Kung Fu, Aikido...

I'm almost invincible

As long as I am on my guards

And that I do my best

It's gonna be okay

I have killed millions of demons already

Alone, my sword cannot make me victorious

It is also prayers and exorcisms

For it is God in us who is invincible

Don't forget your value:

You were made an image of God

It is God who kills the most demons

For 19 years now, I have been fighting evil

All the time, even in my sleep

I received several injuries

It's part of the job

But I gained resistance to pain

Attack the wickedness of the ungodly

Attack evil sudden terrors!!!

Kill the evil man in you (in the invisible)

Hit the devils before they get you

And in general, we are all allergic to evil

Tips for being just:

Fight hard to stay fair

Stay in the light

Walk in the Ways of Justice

Always do good and do your best all the time

Be at peace with the good people

And with those who are for God

Do justice to the weak, the humble and the poor

Deliver the oppressed

Protects the widow and orphan

Believe in God's love

And in the love of truth

Be ready to shed to the last drop of your blood for your beloved wife

Be like a knight

Protect the good ones that are weak

Against the evil that are powerful

Crush the demons that attack God

Be willing to sacrifice your life for God

Cut thorns and thistles and other bad trees

Bear good fruit

Don't harden your heart

Fight Satan only

Turn away from evil

And above all

Worship only God Alone!

Protect God's angels and archangels

Attack the evil beast that the wicked men have followed and worshipped

 The End

Author's Afterword

I wrote this book to talk about what I did for God in the invisible, but also to inspire as many people as possible to fight evil in the invisible reality.

For the wise according to this world, who do not know that there is a God, this book will be folly. But for true Christians, it will be of great use. When the evil in the world will be entirely destroyed, there will be no more wars, sufferings, famines or crimes. Then only will the world become truly a paradise, a place where life is good to live for all those who will have stood firm to the end to be saved. The more the evil is destroyed, the better the world will be, for all those who love the good. This is a very difficult struggle for true Christians because evil is very powerful in this world, and each one of us has to fight many enemies stronger than Ourselves. May this book increase the ranks of those who fight evil in all its forms, for the Glory of God and the salvation of the world!